Cancer

THIS BOOK BELONGS TO:

_____

THE WONDERFUL WORLD OF ZODIACS

Mimi Jones

Dedicated to my son, Mars.

All rights reserved.
No part of this book may be reproduced in any form or by any means, electronic or mechanical, and no photocopying or recording, unless you have written permission from the author.

ISBN 978-1-958985-51-9

Text copyright © 2025 by Mimi Jones

www.joeysavestheday.com

A Mimi Book

WELCOME TO: THE WONDERFUL WORLD OF ZODIACS

IV · CANCER

Mimi Jones

Dates:

Cancer spans from June 21 to July 22.

Ruling Planet:

The Moon rules Cancer.

Symbol:

The Crab represents Cancer.

Cancer

Personality:

Cancers are known for being nurturing and intuitive.

Strength:

They are very empathetic and loyal.

Weakness:

Cancers can be moody and overly sensitive.

Color:

Their lucky colors are white and silver.

Lucky Numbers:

2, 7, 11, and 16 are lucky for Cancers.

Compatibility:

Cancer gets along well with Scorpio, Pisces, Taurus, and Virgo.

SCORPIO

PISCES

TAURUS

VIRGO

Likes:

Cancers love comfort, family, and emotional connections.

fAmILy

Career:

They excel in careers that require compassion and creativity.

Negative Trait:

Sometimes, they can be a bit too clingy.

Cancer

Motto:

Their motto is "I feel."

it's okay to feel your feelings

Favorite Day:

Monday and Saturday are their favorite days.

MONDAY

&

SATURDAY

Health:

Cancers should take care of their stomach and chest.

Hobbies:

They enjoy cooking, gardening, and spending time with loved ones.

Famous Cancers:

Some famous Cancers include Princess Diana, Kevin Hart, and Elon Musk.

Challenges:

Cancers need to learn to manage their emotions effectively.

Friendship:

They are deeply caring friends who will always be there for you.

Feel Deeply

Influence:

They inspire others with their empathy and creativity.

INSPIRE OTHERS

CANCER

Favorite Activities:

Cancers love activities that involve bonding and nurturing.

Birthstones:

The birthstones for Cancer are ruby and pearl.

> If this Zodiac gem tickled your celestial fancy, then you're in for a treat! Dive into my other Zodiac delights right here:
>
> www.mimibooks.com

THE END!

www.ingramcontent.com/pod-product-compliance
Lightning Source LLC
Chambersburg PA
CBHW040030050426
42453CB00002B/64